Copyright © 2014 by Kevin L. Michel

All rights reserved.

No part of this book may be transmitted means, be that electronic, mechanical, pł any format, on any device without the pri lisher. The publisher may be contacted a more information.

...@gmail.com for

The contents of this book are meant to be a mix of the academic and metaphysical, the reader is advised to treat the contents herein as purely theoretical. No method suggested in this book should supersede the advice of one's doctor, therapist or other trained medical professional. The reader is advised to employ caution, practical logic, rationality and common sense when considering any activity suggested in this book. By proceeding to read this book, the reader accepts full responsibility for his or her behavior in spite of any ideas suggested herein. None of the topics in this book should be considered as a substitute for professional advice. The author and publisher specifically disclaim any liability incurred from your use, practice or application of any of the contents of this book.

References to the work and ideas of all individuals mentioned in this book (including, but not limited to scientists, theorists and authors) in no way suggests that these individuals endorse the views or conclusions expressed in this book. The conclusions drawn from all research and quotes in this book are the opinions of the author.

YOUR WORLD

Transform Your Life Instantaneously

By Kevin L. Michel

Also by Kevin L. Michel

Moving Through Parallel Worlds To Achieve Your Dreams: The Epic Guide To Unlimited Power

The Science of Winning Love

Subconscious Mind Power

Subconscious Mind Wealth

Introduction

"The more you say, the less people remember, the fewer the words, the deeper the impression." - François Fenelon

This is your book of concentrated gems. Powerful, transformative ideas that will speed your progress as you move toward achieving all that you desire for yourself. I promise you a powerful book, and I promise you a book that is to the point, although, for effect, at times indirect and subject to your interpretation. I promise that there are powerful ideas in here, and that if you apply the methodology for reading this book, one day at a time, you shall achieve transformative results and phenomenal success with absolute certainty. The book you hold now is the opportunity that you have been seeking. It is the opportunity to do all things and to be all things. It is the opportunity to realize your every dream. Seize this opportunity!

Mov·ing Through Par·al·lel Worlds to A·chieve Your Dreams: The Ep·ic Guide To Un·lim·it·ed Pow·er

1: A book written by Kevin L. Michel that draws on powerful ideas from quantum physics, psychology, biology and behavioral epigenetics to guide the reader on a path to achieving their grandest ambitions.

I·de·al Par·al·lel World

1: The point in your life where all things that you have imagined for yourself have been realized.

2: A future physical world where your 'higher-self' resides. A place where you stand in fullest realization of your potential, and in full connection with your personal power.

3: A point in your future where you achieve a significant accomplishment.

You may have been drawn to this book from having read 'Moving Through Parallel Worlds To Achieve Your Dreams (**MTPW**).' This is most appropriate, for I wrote the majority of the ideas in this book whilst writing **MTPW**. I had notebooks filled with daily insights that I ignored as just random scribblings and never used them, discarding them to a stack of journals that were filled with similar random musings. It was more than a year later, that I returned to consider the contents - now, this book contains the most necessary of these insights. The ideas herein are profound and concise. The ideas are powerful enough to change your life from a single exposure, in a single sitting. The ideas arose from the same inspired place as did MTPW, and as such, this book is inextricably linked to MTPW. Actually, this book cannot be understood without first reading 'Moving Through Parallel Worlds

To Achieve Your Dreams.' It is **not** that this book is a continuation of MTPW, it is that the powerful ideas in this book can only be accessed if one has laid the groundwork through reading MTPW. This book only becomes accessible and intelligible to a person who has read MTPW.

You shall recall that MTPW was a co-creation between us two. It was about you and I coming together to create your personal transformative life insight. For many readers, MTPW was about the inception of the idea that this world we live in is the greatest of all illusions, a game, of which we only experience the elements that are aligned to our subconscious self-concept. For others, it was about embracing the idea that their own subconscious mind was a powerful world shifting force, the greatest supercomputer, capable of navigating a world with dimensions unseen by the conscious mind. And there are as many powerful interpretations and takeaways from MTPW as there are people who read it - each person's interpretation entirely unique and entirely valid in a superposition quite like the many-worlds that make it all possible. But we digress, I would like to suggest, that if indeed you had a positive experience through our co-creation of MTPW then reading this book, '**Your World Shifts**,' is a necessary continuation, a necessary expansion and a necessary refocusing of that experience. **Your World Shifts** is vital for further transforming your thinking and your life, and it shall serve most assuredly to speed your advance to the Ideal Parallel World of your choosing. I invite you to trust me, and join me once again on a journey, in another book that is structured in an untraditional and unfiltered manner. I promise you that every element in this book is set-up to serve your evolution, and your revolution. A book, and method of reading, that is structured in the ideal way to positively alter the very trajectory of your life and get you assuredly, and more hurriedly, on the path to your Ideal Parallel World.

tra·jec·to·ry

1: the curve traveled by a body moving through space.

2: a course, a path, a movement, or line of development that can be likened to the physical movement of a body through space.

3: the cumulative progression of activities that are a part of your life as you move towards your desired ambition that can be likened to the physical movement of a body through space.

Your life is complex, and as human, you are a very complex being, yet all it shall take is an instant to alter the trajectory of your life. Just an instant and you shall begin to move on a more direct trajectory towards a life that is filled with all the fantastical things that you were born to experience.

cha·os the·o·ry

1. the mathematical assessment of complex systems whose behaviors are highly sensitive to slight changes in initial conditions - systems where even the smallest of alterations can lead to strikingly great consequences.

In the midst of struggle we sometimes imagine that to transform our life we must take this gigantic step, this huge leap in another direction, this really big move to something entirely different. Perhaps, sometimes it is like that. But this shift need not be difficult, for you, it shall actually be very simple. What you need is the simplest of ideas to move you onto a more direct track en route to your *Ideal Parallel World*. The simplest of ideas. An idea, that just in assimilating it, moves you onto a newer more direct path to success. All it takes to achieve transformation in the life of an individual is one idea. Just one idea shall shift your world and make all the difference.

but·ter·fly ef·fect

1. a phenomenon accounted for by 'chaos theory,' whereby a minute change in one state of a deterministic nonlinear system has potentially large effects on a later state.

What makes the difference between a man or woman who makes millions of dollars, has a great family and a fun, exciting or peaceful life, and a man or woman who struggles through, meeting failure at many turns, and getting consistently beat up by life? What makes the difference when two kids grow up in similarly difficult neighborhoods, with limited access to resources and support, but one determines himself to rise up and be successful and to build a great career and family and the other fails by embracing the status quo? A single idea, a single approach, a single paradigm, can often be that difference.

"If we are facing in the right direction, all we have to do is keep on walking." ~Proverb

Wonderful people, all over the world, even in the richest of nations, slave away for years, decades, three quarters of a century, and still live in poverty, in mediocrity, and die in poverty and mediocrity. Some do work hard, really. Some do have ambition, really. But work done through the motivated and ambitious mind of someone on the wrong track is just slave labor that ultimately leads to unfulfilling places and unsatisfying rewards. For the path to success is not about being motivated - or at least, that is not the entire story - the path to success is about being motivated in the right direction, on the right trajectory. Your life, shall be a life on the right trajectory, a life that moves in the right direction. Your story shall be one of transformation, abundance and victory, all preceded by your reading of powerful world shifting insights.

METHODOLOGY

This book contains three hundred world shifting ideas - that is more than enough. It may take some readers an entire year to complete. Seemingly, this is not an 'accomplish your goals overnight' book, think of this as an 'accomplish your goals with absolute certainty' book. Maybe it takes you a year to attain the wealth, love, lifestyle or peace that you desire - is this too long a wait? Would you prefer the lottery? Can you wait five years to achieve your dream job and have your dream love and dream life? If you are thinking that five years is too long then let me share the first world shifting idea: *you are going to fail.* Patience and strategy are required for the achievement of all ambitions for *'there are few shortcuts to any place worth going.'* That is just the reality - you shall achieve great things in this life but you must chart your course with powerful intention, planning, purpose and patience.

One of these three hundred ideas in this book is exactly what you need to achieve more rapid success. One of these three hundred ideas is what you need for you to move over to a whole new world, shifting your reality in a way that will astonish those around you. And I reiterate that it is only one of the ideas that is truly what you need, not because they are not all potentially valuable, but because just one of the ideas shall be enough to move you into a reality where you can achieve all that you desire, at which point, you may continue reading, and repeat the process, thus shifting to an even higher level.

So, read only **one** page of this book, every morning when you wake up. Read just one page and think nothing of it, and expect nothing of it. Do not expect to be blown away by the idea - expect nothing. After you read the single, brief page - sometimes a page may be just a sentence, maybe one day it is even just one word - just know that your subconscious mind will dwell on the idea throughout the day. That is all. You cannot rush this process and you cannot judge this process. I have a message for your **con**scious mind that seeks to judge and assess all this, your **con**scious mind that will think some of the ideas are tautological, simplistic, impossible or meaningless, your **con**scious mind that will think it is totally fine to read multiple 'world shifting ideas' in one sitting, I have a message for your **con**scious mind that will question why an entire page on your Kindle should be taken up by the word 'Labrador' or by the un-translated phrase 'labor ipse voluptas,' I have a message for your conscious mind, it is this: "Shut up, go buy a different book, you are not invited, you have no power here." To the real you, the deeper you, the purpose driven fullest expression of you, I offer: "Be willing to give up control and allow this powerful process to unfold."

You see, it is **not** that this book will take 300 days to make a difference or to complete. For one person it may take 300 days to make a huge difference, for another person, the powerful world shifting insight shall be realized after just ten days - but you cannot, and need not rush this process. You cannot read two pages a day to rush the outcome any more than you can force a seed to grow. You cannot rush an idea that is meant to shift your world - you have to allow the shift to happen on its own - you have to trust your subconscious to do the work. You have to be patient and have your conscious mind step out of the way.

Read one world shifting idea every morning after you wake up. Do not judge the idea, do not judge the process. Just allow your **sub**conscious to do the judging. You cannot consciously determine the idea that will shift your world by analyzing it **con**sciously. To analyze an idea **con**sciously is to see if it jives with what you already believe, and by definition, a world shifting idea will be an idea that you do not currently believe, by definition a world shifting idea will be an idea that you will initially reject. But do not reject or accept any of the ideas in this book. Just read the one idea a day, and move on with your life. Do not dwell on it. Just read the idea, and move on. Your subconscious will process, judge, and analyze it from that point forward.

"The significant problems that we face cannot be solved at the same level of thinking we were at when we created them." - Albert Einstein

Be willing to pause and take multiple days, take a week even, and fully apply a particular new idea. For this reason I opted not to put dates on each world shifting idea and instead list them as individual '**DAYS**.' So '**DAY 33**' can last for four days if you want to spend that extra time mentally processing it, and **DAY 62** can last for two days while you work a new idea into your life, and **DAY 204** can last only the twenty-four hours of a normal day if you are ready to move on to the next idea. However, understand that the maximum consumption per day is one page, and this must be applied without exception. Never feel like you must rush through this book. To maximize your benefits from this experience it is important to realize that this cannot be a race.

A single idea shall be what shifts your world. This entire work exists to give you that single idea. That single shifter of your world. That small alteration in your current trajectory that shall change all things for you. You cannot rush through this -- meander through this. Meandering is required to win here.

The world shifting ideas are not grouped into categories based on similarity. Causing a single idea to shift your reality requires an element of surprise, it requires an element of shock. This is better served through chaos than through order. To knock you onto a new trajectory necessarily requires that you be caught off-guard. Your mind shall be busy preparing to shield itself from external input in one direction and then gets struck from a direction for which it was totally unprepared - that is when real shift happens.

"Sometimes when I consider what tremendous consequences come from little things, I am tempted to think there are no little things." - Bruce Barton

Your World Shifts

Your World Shifts is about your transcendence.

Your World Shifts is about taking your potentiality to an entirely new level.

Your World Shifts is about expansion of your awareness.

Your World Shifts is about your further awakening.

Your World Shifts is about adding a new powerful tool to your arsenal of consciousness.

Destiny is often altered by a single idea fully absorbed into the consciousness of an individual. The reading of a single page, a single paragraph, a single line, shall be the instantaneous shift that alters your entire world. This is your opportunity; seize it!

Your World Shifts

DAY 1: That which is required to shift your world and to transform your life is actually the simplest of ideas. Life itself is meant to be simple. The change you must make to achieve all that you desire, the change you must make to shift your world is in fact the simplest of changes. And this therefore is always what you are seeking -- you are seeking a simple change that shall have a multiplier effect, a simple change that shall have an exponential impact -- the flap of the butterfly's wing that shall ripple and rage powerfully, through your entire world.

Now, ask yourself, as it relates to arriving at your Ideal Parallel World, and in handling all circumstances:

"WHAT IS THE SIMPLEST CHANGE I CAN MAKE TO ACHIEVE THE GREATEST IMPACT?"

DAY 2: Do certain work exclusively in certain places and avoid mixing your places. Create a place where you only do a specific type of work related to your purpose - for example specific places for exercise, or study, or practice of a certain type. Whenever you create a new place for work related to a specific aspect of your purpose, you shift worlds.

DAY 3: You have the responsibility, to create each moment and to create each day. You are a creator. Decide in advance how the next moment shall unfold and watch it magically be created into existence. The thought, is the mold that shall create the new world. At the beginning of each day decide in advance how that day shall unfold. These advanced decisions as to how things shall unfold, and what things shall manifest, are immediate shifts in your world regardless of what subsequently occurs. The advanced decision to have the day unfold in a certain manner immediately changes that day and immediately shifts your world.

DAY 4: Every time you think of doing something for others only because of what you shall receive in return, you shrink your world. This applies most specifically to relations with friends and family but applies even in business matters. For in business and all things, the consequences of positive action cannot always be calculated in advance and one may find that offering to be of service to others, when possible, without a focus on personal gain, can lead to unexpectedly great personal gain. You cannot serve in any capacity without being rewarded in equal or greater capacity.

DAY 5: You will always find that which you seek, so seek responsibly. Intelligent seeking shall bring you closer to your Ideal Parallel World. Can you seek peace in a moment of turmoil? Can you seek relief in a moment of despair? Can you seek compassion in a moment of anger? Can you seek great achievement in an environment of failure? A shift in that for which you seek is a shift in reality.

DAY 6: Being grateful is a prerequisite for being wealthy. Every moment of gratitude puts you more completely on the path to attaining great wealth. To be grateful is to bring focus to the resources at your disposal and as such gratitude is an acknowledgement of your present power. You move wealth into your world through gratitude.

DAY 7: Can you be motivated in an instant? Your emotions are key to creating new worlds. Every shift in emotion is a shift in your world. Every positive shift in your emotion brings you closer to your Ideal Parallel World. Today, practice shifting your emotions in an instant, and in each instant realize that in a very real way, your life was just altered.

DAY 8: One of the most important things to your career success is consistently being in the room with the right people. Think from this perspective: "How can I master the art of getting in the right room, at the right organization, regardless of the specific job? Who are the people in the room with those who are most influential? What would it take to be a regular in that room?"

DAY 9: Change in posture is a change in your world. Look at the posture of people when they win. Look at your own posture when you are winning. Learn to mimic that posture when you need to shift into the world of success.

DAY 10: Shift focus, shift worlds. Control your gaze in every moment. The thoughts you focus on impact the world you find yourself in, and affect all future worlds you shall create. A single focused thought is an act of world creation.

DAY 11: Realize that you already know what it takes to shift your world. You already know all that you need to achieve your dreams. You already know everything you need to know to accomplish your goals. You will learn even more, but know that you already know enough. Pause for a moment, think, decide, and then act.

DAY 12: A failure or a drop in performance is actually an opportunity to rise up more powerfully. In weight-lifting, all growth comes from muscle failure at some level – all growth comes from microscopic tearing of muscle fibers and temporary muscle damage, causing initial muscle weakness before repair and growth begins. So should it be odd that when you feel most beaten up by life, you are in fact poised for your greatest growth. Know this, accept this, and you shift your world.

DAY 13: There is both sunlight and darkness ahead, and you must approach both with the same clarity and strategy and certainty. Know that there shall be a time, even if such is not until your very end, a time when you shall be weaker in all faculties than you are today. There may even be a time, near the end, or in misfortune, where you are poorer than you are today. Prepare for all things. Build networks of support and love and savings when you are well and use this positive build-up to secure your future and to help those who are most loyal to you with the acknowledgement that one day the tables will turn.

Similarly, know that your current suffering, if any, is not permanent, and that like the tide, such shall recede, and that your opportunity to arrive at your Ideal Parallel World shall avail itself in time. For neither prosperity nor failure shall be your permanent condition in this world.

DAY 14: You have the power to change the story about any situation. Changing the past story changes your present and future worlds. But is it right or wrong or sane or crazy to change the story of the past? Your world = Your rules.

DAY 15: Asking the right question shifts your world. Ask yourself right now, and know that the answers shall arise during the day: "What is required to elevate your life experience? What is required to give you the **ENERGY** to shift your world?"

DAY 16: If you fail to do something that you are required to do in order to achieve success, it means that at least momentarily, you thought about **NOT** doing it instead of focusing all your thinking on doing it. Do you see how this is an example of negative thinking in your life?

DAY 17: You determine the world you shall move toward. Ask yourself: "What shall it take to arrive at the world you desire?" Then go silent, and wait, and know that the answers are coming.

DAY 18: Today is your day. This is your time. Realize that you are at a pivotal moment and that successful functioning, and brilliant execution in this moment shall bring to you all that you desire. Be brilliant in this moment. Bring your all into this moment, and then repeat the process.

DAY 19: Embrace change. Indeed, this is a common idea that is easy to take for granted, but find opportunities in your day to do things differently for its own sake. The mere act of adjusting to change of any kind develops your mental muscles and helps you to see opportunities to make change in areas where it really matters.

There are future changes in your routine that would lead to increased productivity, changes in the way you interact with others that would lead to better results, changes in the way you approach challenging situations. Practicing the art of adapting to change in small matters will prepare you for dealing with change in important matters. It is certain that you shall require change to arrive at your Ideal Parallel World and a shift in your world is the very definition of change.

Master the skill and art of adapting and responding to change.

DAY 20: The questions you ask must be geared towards arriving at your Ideal Parallel World. The questions you ask must be geared towards achieving your purpose. Such is the real measure of the usefulness of any question.

DAY 21: Your past is whatever you decide it shall be. It is as malleable as the future. Use the 'misinformation effect' to your advantage.

DAY 22: Every word that you speak is a shaper of the world that appears before you. Every word that you speak is itself a creator with world changing effects and powers.

The conjunction 'can't,' the word 'try,' the word 'impossible,' and many similarly restrictive words train and drain your energy. The word 'impossible' is often accurate when used, because it is self-fulfilling. Shift your language and you shift your world.

DAY 23: Gratitude shall reveal to you your infinite wealth. Give thanks for things before they manifest. Give thanks for things to cause them to manifest.

DAY 24: The activities that comprise your life have ripple effects throughout the universe, throughout space-time, and alter all things. The improvements you make to yourself matter, significantly. They affect those around you and they affect the entire cosmos. Through daily improvement, and daily growth, you affect not just your own world but the worlds of everyone else. Choose your activities responsibly.

DAY 25: Be willing to be fired from your job. Be willing to quit your job. Have a plan always for what your job search would be if you were fired and build an understanding of what other job opportunities exist, and if you see a better opportunity, take it. Keep this thinking always to yourself, but employ it nonetheless. Even better, save and learn to create your own investments and even your own small business to ultimately create your own job. The paradox here is that you will be more quickly promoted, more successful and more secure in your current job because you do not cling to it.

DAY 26: There is indeed some work you can do right now, right at this very moment, to move you closer to your Ideal Parallel World. There is work that you can do right now, to begin the process of the fulfillment of your purpose. There is work that you can do right now, that shall bring you closer to that which you desire most. Stop reading, stop what you are doing in this moment, and do that work, now.

DAY 27: Reflect on those who help you to achieve great things and thank them at every possible occasion. To genuinely thank another for their contribution instantly moves you closer to your Ideal Parallel World and it instantly draws in others who shall rally to help you in future endeavors.

DAY 28: Because thought creates your future reality, you must choose your thoughts carefully. Your thoughts create your Ideal Parallel World, and your thoughts move you bodily into your Ideal Parallel World.

DAY 29: Fear arises from illusion – the illusion that the world which is already manifest has more power and reality than the world you are about to create.

DAY 30: If you must dwell on things, dwell on your successes. If you must worry, then worry about how awesome and filled with potential that you are. Worry that you might have even more abundance than you might have imagined when you arrive at your Ideal Parallel World. What are you going to do with all that money, wealth and time and health? So much abundance! If you must worry, worry only about abundance and excess.

DAY 31: Act like a winner for the next few moments. Shift your posture, shift your words, shift your thinking for a moment. Try that winner coat on. Put it on, and walk around the house. This shifts your world.

DAY 32: Your attempt to learn all things will ensure that no one thing is mastered. Use focus and develop expertise. Mastery of tasks in the physical realm, always with an eye towards your purpose, helps you to gain resources you can use to shift your world.

DAY 33: There is sufficient time in the breaks of your day for you to become an expert in the area that best serves the realization of your purpose – so long as you are consistent and persistent. Choose your area of expertise wisely and let it be in a field or trade that you can persist in for the majority of your life. Depending on just how consumed you are by your daily labor, it may take as much as ten years to become a paid expert in your chosen interest – however with more free time and focus it can be in as little as one to five years. Know that such an interval is not as far away as you imagine. Those years shall fly by before you realize it and in all this time you can still be carrying on with the normal activities of day to day living and day to day entertainment. To stay focused every day on developing an area of expertise related to your purpose, is to be a world shifter.

DAY 34: Save. Every day. Save. It is the most important thing you can do to free yourself from being a slave to the wage of your employer. Your savings shall allow you to invest in a yet unseen business or career opportunity. Saving shall allow you, very soon, to seize back control of your time – for you are best able to shift worlds when you are in control of your time.

DAY 35: Every day you **MUST** learn something new. Your knowledge must grow and advance every day. Know where your expertise must be a decade hence, and advance to it with the action of daily learning. Before the day has ended, recount the learning you have done and be sure that you have made progress. This is the manner by which you shall achieve expertise, mastery and advancement. Daily learning is daily movement towards your Ideal Parallel World.

DAY 36: You shall never be wise if you believe that you are wise. Advance every day towards wisdom, and mastery, knowing all the while that you shall never arrive at its doorstep.

DAY 37: Do not seek to be great if you are unwilling to enjoy the process.
Learn to enjoy your work for its own sake.
Find inherent pleasure in the tasks required to shift to your Ideal Parallel World.
If you think the journey to greatness is filled with unpleasantness, do not even bother.

DAY 38: When against the wall, ask this question: "How can I turn this challenge into an opportunity?" This is the essence of judo.

DAY 39: Realize, that exercise makes more things possible. Exercise expands your energy and your potential. The time you spend exercising provides you with more time in the future than it took you to complete each exercise. Time spent exercising multiplies itself in future periods of health, wellness and clearer thinking. It is almost impossible to waste time by exercising too much so long as such exercise is leading to improvements in energy and physical appearance. The time spent shall repay itself in multiplied time, physical well-being and increased financial income. Exercise shifts your world.

DAY 40: You have this moment. You can raise your frequency, and dance, or you can fail to achieve your dreams. To 'dance' in this moment, is to shift your world.

DAY 41: Your view of the world, your perceptions and your paradigms create the energy of your life. Your world is created through your ideas, perceptions and paradigms.

DAY 42: You, are capable, of great patience. Strategy is only possible through the passage of time. Strategy is only made possible through patience. Have a definite vision of the next stage ahead for you, and, wait, patiently, for, your, opportunity, to, emerge. Wait for the right time to take action. Without patience you shall be made bankrupt before arriving at your Ideal Parallel World. Without patience you may even face death. Decide, visualize, plan and strategize, and then execute patience.

DAY 43: Think of each thought of gratitude as a five minute boost of energy that will serve to help you achieve your purpose.

DAY 44: Have a progress report at the end of every day. Ask critical questions: What did I learn today? How did I grow today? What could I have done today to grow at a faster rate? What could I have done to learn more today? Will I face some of the situations from today again in the future, and if so, how can I handle the scenario more appropriately next time around?

DAY 45: The entire universe exists in your own mind. There is not a single person or organism on the planet that shares your perception of reality. Therefore you are the one with the most power to change your world.

DAY 46: Practice the art of keeping your grandest goals and ambitions entirely to yourself. For the involvement of others who see you as you have been in the past is to risk pulling your own self down from your highest future ideals back to the level of accomplishment that represents your history.

DAY 47: Reflect on a moment of victory in your life and use that energy to feel powerful in this moment.

DAY 48: Use your intuition today – it is like a muscle.

DAY 49: Practice the art of predicting the future, for this is a skill that can be improved. Write down your prediction and your basis for the prediction and compare it with how things actually unfold. Then ask: 'What could you have done to have made a better prediction?'

DAY 50: Visualize the method required to achieve success. Visualize yourself completing the required steps. See yourself winning. To see the victory is to instantly shift your world.

DAY 51: You must sometimes battle the dragon alone to gain the fullest understanding.

DAY 52: We worry so much. We worry about things that never come to pass. Tragedies that never befall us. Avoid the worry and avoid the suffering by having an intention as to how you desire events to unfold, and embracing the inevitability of realizing that intention.

DAY 53: I will not love someone who is reckless with my affection.

DAY 54: I choose not to have the time for this.

DAY 55: Everything is linked to everything else, by definition. All causes lead to all effects. You are most certainly responsible for the events that comprise your life. Embrace this, and you shift your world.

DAY 56: Know what your Ideal Parallel World looks like and ensure that no matter how much you are pushed around and moved over, that you stay focused on it, and keep moving forward.

DAY 57: All matter is working to ensure that you reach your Ideal World. Even the seeming obstacles are working to strengthen you so that you do arrive at your Ideal World.

DAY 58: If you allow sloth and vice to pull you away from your path to the Ideal Parallel World, you shall not long survive.

DAY 59: Know that all things are conspiring to cause you to realize your purpose. Know that you cannot fail, unless you give up — even still, you shall win.

Day 60: Realize that every moment is part of your journey to greatness. Every moment is a moment of greatness. You are living your dream at this very moment.

Day 61: There is no suffering in the pursuit of one's dream. Only joy and bliss and certainty. For even the suffering is joyful suffering, blissful suffering and certain suffering.

Day 62: Get control of your energy. Get control of your thoughts. Spend each moment directing your joy to that which you intend to reinforce. Love the habits that serve your growth.

Day 63: The journey to achieving one's dream is a journey of joy and bliss and certainty.

Day 64: Others may not be able to see that which you are about to create – nor must they.

Day 65: Only fear can make your dreams unattainable.

Day 66: It shall be the words you speak to yourself, that is, your own thoughts, which will determine your destiny. Let these thoughts be thoughts of ambition and thoughts about ways to make things happen. Let these thoughts be thoughts of persistence in spite of obstacles. Let these thoughts be a knowing that you shall be victorious in the end and then you shall move assuredly to this inevitable outcome of victory. This life is your story. You are the hero who wins in the end but also the hero who faces ups and downs and all manner of battles and challenges yet wins it all in the end.

DAY 67: When you improve, the world improves.

DAY 68: Life shall pay you that which you believe is fair – do not settle for less or sell yourself short.

DAY 69: When you accept that you can achieve the improbable, you shift worlds.

DAY 70: In the area of your life where your purpose lies, you must apply 'Heisenberg standards' at all times.

DAY 71: Be more organized. Step into the 'frame of organization,' the 'mindset of organization' where for a set period of time you bring more order and structure to everything you encounter.

DAY 72: Network. Get to know people. Find opportunities to connect. Enter 'the frame of networking' where you focus on ways to strengthen your key connections in every moment.

DAY 73: If you had not lived, the very universe would be altered.

DAY 74: All things are not perfect with your life. You are not yet at your Ideal Parallel World. Consider how you can enjoy the journey to your Ideal Parallel World. Consider how you can find joy in the current apparent imperfections of your world. For there will always be imperfections, even at your Ideal Parallel World there shall be imperfections. Learning to enjoy the journey is learning therefore to live a life of happiness.

DAY 75: If you have a sedentary job, seek every opportunity you can to add more physical effort to your work. Walk around the room randomly, get out of your chair to reach for things, take the long way on foot to wherever it is you are heading. It will make you less productive for a week, but your body will adjust, and every week, repeating this approach, you shall expand your potential.

DAY 76: Strategize often. Practice strategizing.

DAY 77: Stand back and observe frequently. When you take a moment to assess your reality, you shift your world.

DAY 78: Seek every opportunity to find pleasure in the work you do. Enjoy the work for its own sake. See the inherent joy in every step on the way to your Ideal Parallel World. In so doing you clear the path ahead.

DAY 79: Labor ipse voluptas.

DAY 80: Work today as though the achievement of that which you desire most is at stake — it is.

DAY 81: Realize there is power in patience. Move steadily in your chosen direction. The road to wealth and success is long, but for you, it is certain. Arrival at your Ideal Parallel World is certain.

DAY 82: Allow the current illusion of reality to dance. Allow the current illusion, that is, your current world to have fun with itself. Know that you shall create your Ideal World and that your Ideal World is the greatest reality.

DAY 83: Learn to enjoy the magnificent growth you can achieve over time.

DAY 84: Where it comes to personal study every day is Groundhog's Day. You get to do each day again, and you get to keep the lessons you learned from the day prior. Realize, that in this game of reality, that every day is like "The Edge of Tomorrow."

DAY 85: Create a plan for the next year, and the next five years. Post that plan somewhere you shall see it every day.

DAY 86: Do not accept any negative fate. Do not embrace any undesirable destiny. Do not feel trapped by any current position. Accept only that you exist in this world to achieve your chosen purpose.

DAY 87: Your words and your desires in any moment

might be saying that you would like to live a life of abundance and achieve great things and afford to travel the world and spend time with those you love, and this is great. It is great that in your thoughts and words you say these things. But, what are your actions saying? Is that third hour of recreational television saying that you are the type of person who can afford to fly on a private chartered jet? Does that two hours a day you spend on social media say that you're the type of person who can afford to stay in the finest hotels in Paris with the people you love? Does that tenth hour of sleep on the weekend say that you want to be able to be chauffeured in the finest cars and get last-minute premium seats to the finest concert events and Broadway shows? Do your actions communicate to the universe, in a manner of speaking, that you are this person who is capable of great things and who should therefore be rewarded with all manner of luxury and support? Take notes today and write down what your actions are actually saying. Maybe your actions are saying that you are comfortable with mediocrity? Maybe your actions are saying that you are okay with the idea of having the person you are most attracted to be with another person who takes them for granted but is significantly more successful? Maybe that's cool for you? Maybe missing out on your dreams is cool? What you must do to shift your world is ask the question in your every moment: "What does this action suggest that I have as my objective?" "What kind of success is achieved by the person who is using their time in a manner like I am doing right now?" Ensure that your actions suggest the type of person who arrives at their Ideal Parallel World. Align your grandest Ideal with your daily actions, and you shall shift your world.

DAY 88: Appreciate that there shall be challenges along the way and that you shall overcome them.

DAY 89: The biggest saboteur in your life is in the version of you attached to your current world. See the saboteur within you, and you shall shift worlds.

DAY 90: The world you inhabit is temporary.

DAY 91: Struggle cannot be permanent for you. Only ease is permanent. Know that the advance to your Ideal World is along the path of ease, and that life in the Ideal Parallel World is a life of ease.

DAY 92: Allow adversity to build your muscle in preparation for your arrival at your Ideal Parallel World.

DAY 93: Know that the variable of time and the inner attribute of persistence are vital to your success.

DAY 94: Failure was and shall continue to be necessary for you to achieve greatness.

DAY 95: Have the patience to master the details. Think long term.

DAY 96: Every creation lasts for eternity. Every moment lasts for eternity. Create with this in mind.

DAY 97: Time spent on creation can be sensed intuitively by others – it all matters.

DAY 98: The more you prepare the stronger shall be your intuition and your ability to adapt to changing situations.

DAY 99: Craft a model for exponential growth. If you had to grow a skill, attribute or business exponentially, what strategies would you use? Think about it.

DAY 100: Action is required to make the move to your Ideal Parallel World, but ensure that it is inspired action – action that is driven by the higher-self, action that is determined by the subconscious as necessary to shift to the Ideal Parallel World. You shall know that it is inspired action because it is effortless.

DAY 101: There is no committee gathering right now that is seeking ways to advance you and seeking ways to get you to arrive at your Ideal Parallel World. Few or none of us have the great fortune of some amazing benefactor walking up to us and giving us the opportunity that moves us closer to achieving our dreams. It is your responsibility to create the openings and opportunities in your career and your life. Build a network of supporters, yes, but know that only you can save yourself.

DAY 102: Keep visualizing success and the steps required for success. See yourself taking every step with ease. To visualize success, even for a brief moment, is to shift your world.

DAY 103: You must move or you shall be stuck in the present world. Activity shall be required to achieve that which you desire. Guidance shall come to you in your moments of silence as to the type of activity that is needed.

DAY 104: Decide that today is the day you shift worlds.

DAY 105: There is one great force to which you are connected. Know that you are one with all things and can see through the eyes of all things. To know this is to instantly shift worlds. Practice the art of seeing through the eyes of another human – anticipating their next move by seeing from their perspective. For you are the other person.

DAY 106: Do not hope to achieve great things if all you seek are the physical pleasures of this reality, unless you can derive such pleasure from the practice and training required to achieve greatness. Only when you are able to find pleasure from the tasks required to achieve greatness, shall you shift worlds.

DAY 107: Procrastination is a great danger. Take every action you can once you come to know the type of action that is required.

DAY 108: Once you are engaged in activity that moves you towards achieving that which you desire most, even indirect action, you can only feel joy. Take action and remember to be joyful in so doing.

DAY 109: You have the ability to change your emotion in any moment, and a shift in emotion is always a shift in worlds. Small shifts when magnified over time, make all the difference.

DAY 110: It is all uncertainty, unless you choose the path of certainty. To know what your Ideal World looks like and to move confidently in that direction, is to choose the path of certainty.

DAY 111: Be open and willing to take a different path to arrive at your Ideal World. The path will never be the exact path you imagined but the arrival at your destination will be as imagined. Just trust and adjust.

DAY 112: Repeating the right behaviors is key to success. What are some right behaviors you sometimes engage in? How can you make such behaviors more frequent?

DAY 113: It is acceptable to mentally change the facts of a past experience. You are allowed to believe whatever you want to believe. Really.

Be willing to shift the meaning of past experiences. Ask yourself, 'Is there any experience in your past that you would like to re-write?' Go for it!

DAY 114: Worry not. For all obstacles shall move aside

once you advance confidently to your Ideal Parallel World.

DAY 115: The further you advance along the road to your Ideal Parallel World the greater shall be your ability to shine light on the path ahead.

DAY 116: Every moment of every day realize that there is a gentleman working to destroy your Ideal Parallel World. His name is Inertia — and he does not stop working against you. You should stop reading this and get back to working on your move to the Ideal World, for Inertia takes no breaks and he will be happy to sleep with the one you love most and burn down your house and take the food off your plate and have you living in squalid conditions. Inertia wants to destroy you and ultimately have you killed. He is working without cessation, and you need to be more productive and efficient than he is if you intend to arrive at your Ideal World.

DAY 117: Everything you desire exists. Your Ideal World already exists. Having the person you desire most is already a certainty. The only question is whether or not you are going to be outworked by Inertia. Do not let Inertia outwork you — he is working right now. He will destroy your Ideal World.

DAY 118: Fight Inertia. Take a step right now to get ahead of him. Take a bold step towards your Ideal World.

DAY 119: Know that causality is at work in your life. Know that cause and effect is relevant and that if you focus every day on improving your abilities with an eye towards your purpose, that your success is inevitable.

DAY 120: Each moment must be cherished for you shall have only this moment.

DAY 121: Make it a habit of doing good for others, whilst expecting nothing in return. Generosity shifts your future possibilities. The question is not 'how can you be loved?' the question is 'how can you love?'

DAY 122: Death is in your future. Seize life now. Do it now. Winter is coming.

DAY 123: All positive things in your present reality must be celebrated and enjoyed – this shall make the journey more pleasurable and shall give you energy to persist. Gratitude and love are the energy you need to persist in your journey to your Ideal World.

DAY 124: Failure is a part of the journey to success – this is guaranteed and must be celebrated and embraced with the knowing that such failure is temporary.

DAY 125: There are great challenges up ahead, and the path shall look daunting, but you must know that every day you shall grow stronger and more able. You shall become greater than any obstacle that comes before you. You shall have intellectual breakthroughs, you shall innovate, you shall strategize, you shall win. Do not ask the universe for an easy journey, ask for the strength to face those great challenges ahead, and the strength shall be provided.

DAY 126: The world you are about to create has more power and reality than the world that is before you in this moment.

Choose to see past the illusion of the present moment.

Practice seeing past the illusion of the present moment.

DAY 127: Keep moving forward, especially after taking a step back.

DAY 128: A key to arriving at your Ideal World is organization and strategy. See just how organized you can be.

See just how many steps ahead of life and circumstances you can be. Ask yourself, 'what is going to happen next?' 'How can you prepare for this?'

DAY 129: What in the present moment are you doing to strengthen your financial position for retirement? What is your plan for having money to retire? Are you willing to strengthen your financial situation over time instead of hoping or wishing?

DAY 130: In the absence of another, speak well of them or speak nothing at all. To decide now that you shall set this as your new standard is to immediately shift worlds.

DAY 131: There are basic rules to create financial abundance. Learn them. It all starts with saving.

DAY 132: You are creating your future world – accept this now and move forward.

DAY 133: Your brain is wired to reject new ideas – know that this is true and actively become more open to new ideas.

Day 134: You created the Universe – act like it.

Day 135: You can earn increasing wealth if you keep increasing your value to humanity. Your compensation shall match the value of your contribution to this species.

Day 136: As in all heros' journeys, there shall be a point in pursuit of your purpose where your ambitions will be met with certain death. All your hopes shall hang by the thinnest of lines, you shall be dangling over the chasm of despair and shall only then make a leap to success.

Day 137: You are greater, stronger and wiser than you realize. You can decipher this maze of life, you shall reach your Ideal Parallel World.

Day 138: Every activity that you do shall be improved upon in future time – so you should think from this perspective and find ways to do your work better today. Realize improvements are coming, imagine what they shall be, and do them now.

Day 139: That which is occurring to you now, that which you may perceive as misfortune, the opportunity which seems to have been denied to you, is actually serving your interests in the long term. Remain focused on the realization of your purpose and all shall be revealed to you in the long-run.

Day 140: Increase your abilities every day and see the tremendous shift in your life after one year.

Day 141: Approach that which you desire with certainty.

Day 142: Focus on the area that is your passion. Focus. Be the best in your area.

Day 143: It's not about how the people in your life can make you happy. It is about how can you make the people in your life happy. It is not about how your dad, or aunt, or best friend, or lover can make you happy. That must not be the focus of your time and energy. The focus of your time and energy must be on how you can make them happy. The focus of your time and energy must not be what value you can get from your friends — your focus of your time and energy must be, what value can you give to your friends.

DAY 144: Take time today to write down the many factors that are conspiring to guarantee your success — and here is a hint... all factors are conspiring. Write down the ways in which these factors are conspiring and how each of them serves your advancement.

DAY 145: Begin to be now that which you shall become.

DAY 146: Look away from that which appears to bring riches overnight. Focus on long-term growth.

DAY 147: Every reading of these world shifting ideas shall bring you new and different insights.

DAY 148: Make the decision to grow your business. Make the decision to earn more money. It is as simple as deciding on the world you intend to create and making progressive moves toward it in every moment that you can. It is easy to move to your Ideal World once you have clarity.

DAY 149: You are entirely responsible for the current structure of your world. The reality that is unfolding around you is entirely your doing and your action or distraction, will determine your future worlds.

DAY 150: Ensure that your inner monologue is in line with the person you are at your Ideal Parallel World.

DAY 151: Criticism is welcomed. Listen and learn from it. Know that criticism is as valuable as praise.

DAY 152: Do not fear that there will be obstacles ahead, for the only possible obstacles are in your own mind. Your seeing yourself as permanently attached to your present world is the only possible obstacle.

DAY 153: Accept responsibility for where you are. Accept responsibility for who you are. Accept responsibility for what you earn. Once you fully accept responsibility, you access the power to shift your world.

DAY 154: Direct your passion with caution. Abandon yourself in the right direction. Get lost on the right path.

DAY 155: Risk is required to find abundance. Deliberately take a risk today, and see what great fun and opportunity can come with it. I am not talking about the lottery, I am talking about sensible and strategic risk-taking, where there is a realistic probability of winning.

DAY 156: Follow your purpose. Make progress and advance over time.

DAY 157: Think on that which you consider to be past failures . . . but before you think on them, step into the personae of the great person you are at your Ideal Parallel World. Now looking back on those so called failures, do you now see how they actually served your purpose, and how they in fact have value, and needed to occur to get you on the right path? Do you see how you were stuck in those failures until you learned the required lessons to advance beyond them? Yes.

DAY 158: Practice seeing past the illusion of the present. Practice seeing wealth where there is poverty. Practice seeing health amidst illness. Practice seeing competence when you are still an amateur. Practice seeing day when it is still night. This is the sight you need, this is a skill that is vital in shifting over to your Ideal World. For you must see wealth to create wealth, you must see health to create health, you must see competence to become competent, you must see the day to persist through the night.

DAY 159: Passionately enjoy that which is required to achieve success. It is in the practice and preparation that you must find the greatest joy.

DAY 160: Today is a day of adventures. Be sure to write down all the exciting things that occur, for there shall be many. Write them all down now — write them down before your day has even begun . . . intend to make today a day of personal/professional adventures.

DAY 161: When you've got great momentum, do not stop.

DAY 162: Just by having a goal and advancing every day, you are a tremendous success.

DAY 163: Know why you do what you do. Use that 'why' to lift yourself up in the darkest times; use that 'why' to stay focused when things are going well; use that 'why' to rally others to your cause.

Day 164: There is still work you can do to be an even more effective reader and student. Reading and studying is a skill that can be improved throughout life. Improving your reading and study skills is an immediate 'leveling up' in the game of life.

Day 165: There are no exterior forces that determine your destiny. You are the shaper of your future worlds. Now, is this literally true? Do you in fact control your external environment? The answer regarding literal truth is irrelevant – what is most certain, is that the smaller your perceived locus of control, the less you shall notice when your actions are creating effects. To see the world from the perspective of unlimited power, is to gain progressive access to unlimited power.

Day 166: Creating a clear vision of your Ideal Parallel World, immediately focuses you and shifts you into a new world.

Day 167: For you, defeat is always temporary. You win in the end, and as such, every defeat serves your growth once you are aware that future growth is the very purpose of every defeat. This is all just combat training.

DAY 168: Your thoughts are creating. Your dominant thoughts shape your future worlds. Focus on saturating yourself with thoughts of advancement.

DAY 169: A shift in attitude is a shift in worlds. Learn to shift.

DAY 170: People fear the new. Be subtle, be strategic. Even when you achieve genius people shall find ways to fear and malign you. Be subtle, so your ideas can fully take hold before people realize that a change has occurred. Big change is best executed subtly.

DAY 171: Do you think from the perspective of prosperity?

DAY 172: Do not wait for opportunity to knock. Hunt down and seize opportunity wherever it may be. Now say it: "I do not sit timidly and wait for opportunity to knock. I am the one who knocks!'"

DAY 173: When we lack clarity about what our Ideal World looks like we have fear, doubt and disbelief.

Day 174: The more you follow your purpose in spite of obstacles, the more opportunities that shall avail themselves to continue to allow you to follow your purpose. Think long term, and move steadily in the right direction.

Day 175: Taking risk does NOT mean that you go jumping off cliffs without support. Taking risks means you continually push yourself out of your comfort zone in pursuit of your dreams.

Day 176: Ask yourself for the adventure of the day/week/month and go for it. Have these short term adventures frequently. This is great practice for moving outside your comfort zone.

Day 177: Time is one of the physical dimensions of this reality, and for your success it is a powerful ally. Time is a great equalizer. Through the strategic usage of time all things are possible for you. Strategic usage of time allows you to shift worlds. Next time you are faced with a challenge or a battle, ask yourself: "How can I use time to achieve a victory?" This is the same question you must ask to arrive at your Ideal Parallel World.

Day 178: In the mirror lies all your answers. That one in the mirror is creating your world.

Day 179: You can have truly enduring success if you always hold yourself accountable for the manner in which things unfold. You do not need to control all things, you just need to understand that your performance is enough to alter all things.

Day 180: If you intend to transform the world, you need to find joy in the activities that will make you so capable — you need to enjoy the practice, you need to enjoy sharpening the saw, you need to enjoy the necessary work. You must find **THE MOST** pleasure from the work required. I have to be clear on this — you can passionately enjoy all manner of hedonistic and entertaining things, but you must derive **THE MOST** pleasure from the work, from the study, from the practice, from your training. This shall ensure that you stay focused throughout your advance. Thus, "labor ipse voluptas," is your key to all achievement.

Day 181: Step into the mindset of already being the version of yourself who lives in your Ideal World. Be that great self now.

DAY 182: You are the creator of your own myth. You are the creator of your own story. This is what it is to find 'meaning' in your life – the way to find meaning is to create it. Write up the story of your own life, most certainly with yourself as the hero, and then live it!

DAY 183: Save a **MINIMUM** of ten percent of your income, no matter how small or great it may be. Significantly more important than the sum actually saved, is the 'habit of saving.'

DAY 184: Until you master the art of drawing unlimited power to yourself, which is achievable in the infinity of your lifetimes – you shall start each day with a set amount of energy. You must therefore be very careful how you spend that energy and ensure that you are investing your time in the areas that shall yield the most value.

DAY 185: You are the source of power in the Universe. Yes indeed, that is a big statement. Accept it. Know it. Recognizing this power allows you to more effortlessly shift your world. It allows you to see how all things are conspiring to create your success.

DAY 186: You can lift yourself up and become so high

and focused and energetic, that you can achieve in one hour what it takes others days to accomplish. Know that this is true and pursue it. In your world, time runs differently.

DAY 187: Do not expend your energy on petty things. All things are petty that do not serve your purpose.

DAY 188: Focus on the handful of activities that yield the greatest positive benefit in your life. Focus on the handful of activities that serve the accomplishment of your purpose.

DAY 189: You success shall be achieved through the support of many and can be celebrated with many, but loss must always be owned by you alone. Accept any losses on the road to your Ideal Parallel World with complete grace. This shall prepare you for the next stage of advancement.

DAY 190: You achieve your greatest power when you become trusting of your inner voice.

DAY 191: The opinions of others are always secondary.

DAY 192: You can have any attribute you so desire – all

you need do is ask, step into it, and persist in acting.

DAY 193: Even in silence you are communicating. Even in silence you are drawing some things toward you and pushing some things away. Your subconscious is constantly working – ensure that you are always planting the right ideas in your subconscious.

DAY 194: That which affects your mood affects your body. Learn to raise your mood in all circumstances. See clearly, confront obstacles when you must, but do so with the greatest clarity and with the highest levels of joy that you can achieve.

DAY 195: Intend to have the energy you need to achieve success. That intention is enough.

DAY 196: Intend to find joy in that which serves the realization of your purpose. That intention is enough.

DAY 197: What are micro-expressions?

mi·cro ex·pres·sions

1. micro expressions, are facial expressions that last frac-

tions of a second, and occur when an individual either deliberately or unconsciously conceals a feeling. Micro-expressions can sometimes communicate our real intentions or feelings in a manner that leads to self-fulfilling prophecies.

DAY 198: Know that there is great success and abundance in your future. That 'knowing' instantly shifts your world.

DAY 199: Courage is required to attain unlimited power.

DAY 200: Once you realize that every thought you have is a real tangible force, you shall choose to think with greater caution, and you shall be able to create that which you desire most with greater speed.

DAY 201: If you spend time with the weak, you become the weak. We gradually absorb the weaknesses and frailties of mind of those we surround ourselves with, just as a traveller progressively begins to absorb the accents of a foreign town. Time spent with others pulls us into the worlds of those others.

Day 202: If you seek great wealth, spend not a moment being distracted by the coarser things in your current world. Create a plan to arrive at your Ideal Parallel World of greater wealth and stick to it, spending scarcely a moment distracted by coarser things.

Day 203: All suffering in the pursuit of your dream, is illusion.

Day 204: Pleasure is entirely subjective. You can train your mind to perceive orgasmic pleasure from anything. Find a small task related to your work, and practice feeling greater pleasure than normal from engaging in that task, then do this again with a different task, and then again, and then again.

Day 205: You have the power to hypnotize yourself with your own thoughts. First find silence and peace and then communicate an intention to yourself.

Day 206: Have nothing ill to say of another. Choose silence if there is nothing good to be said. Or speak from the perspective of positive action that will be taken to cope with the behavior of another.

DAY 207: You shall face criticism – either use it or lose it – consider it or ignore it. Handle it in an impartial manner separate from your own ego.

DAY 208: Offer more value than your customer expects.

DAY 209: To think from the perspective of your future self is to draw the capabilities of that future self to you now.

DAY 210: In your world there is no failure, for in every apparent miss you shall draw great lessons that will serve your advance to the Ideal World. The only possible failure is a failure to reflect and see the great lessons in the missteps. In reflection, lies the seed of the world shift you most need.

DAY 211: Your belief that greatness is possible is what allows you to achieve greatness. To be open in this instant to greatness, is to instantly shift your world.

DAY 212: Realize that all elements and all forces are working to serve you – practice seeing ways in which you can harness all things to achieve your vision of success.

DAY 213: It takes great courage to move in the direction of that which you desire most. It takes courage to step into the fullness of who you are even before you have arrived, that is, to step into the fullness of who you shall become, right now, in this present moment. But this is what you must do. It takes courage to have a 'knowing.' It takes courage to shift your world. But know that the greatest danger is in not stepping-up and not stepping into your higher-self, right now.

DAY 214: If you fail to move towards your dream in this moment, you will not get a concession prize, you will not be first runner-up, you will not get the bronze medal in life — you will lose, everything. You must act to move toward achieving your Ideal World right now, right in this moment, or you will be annihilated. Get it.

DAY 215: Focus is your key to all power.

DAY 216: Once you learn to focus, all things shall be possible for you . . . but you would not do all things. To focus is to seize control of the world shifting process.

DAY 217: Meditation is a key to shifting worlds. Meditate frequently. Even a minute of meditation powerfully alters your future; even 10 seconds of meditation powerfully alters your future; even one deep breath of meditation is a micro-shift of your world.

DAY 218: Even if you fail repeatedly in pursuit of a goal, you are making progress. Every time you make an attempt, every time you take a new approach, you alter the future, you shift your world.

DAY 219: Keep your vision at the forefront of your mind and enjoy the process. This is a guaranteed path to goal accomplishment.

DAY 220: All the effortful practice required to succeed must be perceived as pleasurable. This is the key to all success.

DAY 221: When you take the advice of someone, even if it is not the best advice, you gain their support in helping you shift worlds. You can always course correct later but this way you shall be course correcting with a supporter helping you along.

DAY 222: Realize that energy will follow action – do not wait for action to follow energy because it rarely does.

DAY 223: The key to avoiding disappointment is to realize that quantum superposition is the outcome of all pursuits. You shall both achieve the goal and NOT achieve the goal simultaneously, in varying degrees based on probability. Ensure in your approach and preparation that you are all set for both outcomes, and you shall find that you will achieve the Ideal outcome.

DAY 224: Your subconscious is not always direct in moving you towards your Ideal Parallel World. Many times it is indirect, many times it puts you in certain situations that are undesirable so that you can build the muscle that comes from finding your way out. That muscle is what is needed to climb higher, to climb into the Ideal Parallel World.

DAY 225: You shall have the energy required to get to the Ideal Parallel World of your choosing. Know that this is true. Know that you shall have all the energy that is needed — but here is an important corollary — you must take action first before the energy is revealed, for the energy shall come from action. See fatigue, exhaustion and desire to procrastinate as saying to you 'time to take the first steps.'

Day 226: The shifts in action required to create perfect health are within you. You are capable of shifting behavior and shifting worlds to arrive at magnificent health and breathtaking wellness. You are an amazing physical specimen, and flawlessly well, at your Ideal Parallel World – get there.

Day 227: It is your purpose and destiny to arrive at your Ideal Parallel World – if you advance confidently, and with focus, you cannot fail to achieve your purpose, you cannot escape your destiny. Your will move to the shore of success with inevitability.

Day 228: You created all things that you perceive as undesirable in your life. You created all these undesirables, and you shall create their inverse.

Day 229: You are able to find all that you perceive as missing in your life. Know this, and instantly, your world shifts.

Day 230: Every moment you focus on your Ideal Parallel World, every moment you clarify your ambitions, your intentions, you make the Ideal Parallel World more real. You create the Ideal World in your mind, and having created the Ideal World in your mind you create a force that is like gravity pulling you towards it.

DAY 231: First you create you Ideal World and then your Ideal World will begin to recreate you.

DAY 232: Find the opportunity right now to do one thing that moves you closer to your Ideal World, do one thing, something that draws you closer. Do a right behavior. Do a right thought. Every iteration, every action, counts. It all matters and all helps draw you to your Ideal World.

DAY 233: Plans will be required to move to the Ideal Parallel World of your choosing, but do not hurry into the planning phase. Be clear about what it is you desire, visualize it, step into the feeling and emotion of it, and then the subconscious shall guide you in the drafting of all plans.

DAY 234: Take a different path to or from work today, and know that by so doing you have just altered your future. Now choose a different thought in a moment of typical weakness or doubt, and know that in the same manner you have just altered your future world.

Day 235: In order to win, you must be willing to lose. Never fear that you shall fail – move boldly, be strategic, be patient, but always be open to some risk. Risk is inherent in all life, in all activity and inactivity.

Day 236: You have an ability that is unlike the ability of anyone who has ever lived. You are truly unique in your world and the contribution you make to humanity that will cause you to arrive at your Ideal Parallel World shall be a truly unique contribution.

Day 237: Focus you energy on service and value creation. This immediately aligns you with your higher-self and creates a real shift in the trajectory of your life – a real movement towards your Ideal Parallel World.

Day 238: Realize that the work you do shall transform this planet, and it shall transform your world.

Day 239: Abundant riches are on their way into your life. Know this, and you shift your world.

Day 240: Pursue joy in each moment. Each experience of joy immediately shifts your world.

Day 241: Your attention and intention are shaping your future worlds. Consider, in this moment, where you are placing your attention and take careful note of your intentions. Ensure attention and intention are predominantly on the creation of your Ideal Parallel World, avoid the short term distractors of your attention and intention.

Day 242: The version of yourself that is at the Ideal World and in full alignment with that which you desire is always present in this moment to guide you. Connect with this higher version of yourself through silence and meditation – and you shall be guided.

Day 243: The way you feel is the best guide to whether you are in alignment with the version of yourself that exists at your Ideal Parallel World. Being in alignment with your highest self is a feeling of happiness, joy, pleasure and bliss.

Day 244: You become that which you focus on – everything you focus on shall be pulled into your world. When you focus on what you do not want you are adding it to your Ideal World, and causing your Ideal World to become less than Ideal.

DAY 245: Stand in the Ideal Parallel World in your visualizations, and in every waking moment you can, only then shall you have the perspective to assess your current circumstance.

DAY 246: Be honest about the strengths, weaknesses, opportunities and threats in your current world. Seeing past the illusion of reality does not mean you act as though you were blind, it means that you see things from a much broader perspective, it means you can handle 'what is,' with an understanding that your current weaknesses and threats are merely that which you ultimately overcome on your path to greatness.

DAY 247: There is a short term desire that shall fall apart — allow it to. You were so sure you wanted it, but alas, it is not part of the highest version of yourself. Allow it to go by knowing that there is a higher level of greatness up ahead for you.

DAY 248: Master your finances. Save aggressively. Opportunities for sensible investment shall emerge down the line and this shall speed your advance to your Ideal World.

DAY 249: Write down that which you intend. Define what the world you intend to manifest looks like. Refer to your description of the Ideal World regularly, and know that you shall create it – know that it already exists and you are moving effortlessly towards it.

DAY 250: Let go of your need to arrive at your Ideal Parallel World whilst remaining focused on arriving at your Ideal Parallel World. This action of reducing attachment to the end result is paradoxical, in that letting go, and separating from outcome, shall actually speed your advance. *"Let it go! Let it go!"*

DAY 251: There is great excitement today. Today you shall advance towards all that you desire. But this post is not about today, it is about every single day of your life. This is the mindset with which every day must be approached. There are things more marvelous and extraordinary today than you can possibly imagine – all you need to do now is move forward and discover them.

DAY 252: Do not force things to work out as you desire. Do not fight, do not flail, do not struggle. Allow the illusion of things to play out. See opportunities in every single situation.

DAY 253: There are solutions and opportunities embed in every challenge. Every challenge prepares you for your advance to your Ideal Parallel World.

DAY 254: You shall be required to take risks to make the move to your Ideal Parallel World – risks are a natural part of this game, this illusion that is reality. Take your risks confidently, knowing that you win in the end.

DAY 255: Your current world is entirely your creation. You created your current world both consciously and unconsciously. Accept this, and you make a move towards unlimited power. Accept this and you shall learn to consciously create your future worlds.

DAY 256: With the illusion of time at play, and the resultant truth that all things occur simultaneously, the Ideal World that you imagine is created the instant you imagine it. Your Ideal World is an instant creation – it is folly to doubt a world that you have already created with your thoughts – it is folly to be afraid that darkness shall prevent you from ever arriving at your Ideal World when such has already occurred. Instead, choose acceptance – acceptance of your inevitable victory, your inevitable creation.

DAY 257: Share the vision of your Ideal Parallel World with no one, or only with the one or few persons who believe in you fully. To do otherwise is to risk the diminishment of your vision and to risk creating resistance to that which you desire most.

DAY 258: Trust your intuition above all else – even above the words on this page – even above this advice telling you to trust your intuition, for sometimes you should not trust your intuition – only your intuition can tell you . . . or can it?

"The angels fly because they take themselves lightly."

Move ahead to DAY 259 tonight – from this day forward, you may read one DAY in the morning, and one DAY before bed at night.

DAY 259: You shall not see the entire path to your Ideal World. To see the entire path is to become dangerously inflexible. Be open to shifts in direction and changes in terrain whilst remaining focused on your Ideal World. So focus on the Ideal, and be inflexible about the Ideal, but be open to a variety of paths and resist no path, for all paths can potentially lead you to the inevitability of your Ideal Parallel World. Put your head down and keep moving towards the Ideal World with certainty.

Day 260: What really gives you a huge instantaneous shift in worlds is imagination. To have imagination is to have power over all circumstances. Applied imagination is the key and allows you to conquer any situation.

Day 261: The common attribute that characterizes all those who arrive at their Ideal Parallel World is relentlessness – a persistent refusal to give in or give up.

Day 262: So much indecision in life is brought on by the mindset that some things are possible for you and some things are not possible – this is what creates the uncertainty. Without this uncertainty the answer to the question: *"What would you like to do with your life?"* becomes so much easier. It is acceptable to be practical, it is acceptable to say that one goal will take longer than another, but even in accessing degree of difficulty we are often wrong – for sometimes pursuing the greater, less probable goal inspires us and motivates us to such an extent that we achieve the improbable victory – whereas with a lesser goal we might even have failed for lack of motivation. All this is to say, decide on what it is you desire, and go for it. And to hell with the people who do not believe. And if you do not believe, then to hell with you. Shut-up, stop dithering, stop thinking about it and go out there and achieve the improbable.

DAY 263: You can tell how aligned you are with your Ideal Parallel World by the nature of your emotions. Feelings of joy, love and gratitude suggest an alignment with yourself at the Ideal Parallel World and feelings of anger, hurt, jealousy suggest a misalignment.

How do you feel in this moment? If you are doing work that is related to your purpose then do whatever it takes to elevate your emotion during that period of time. Find things to be joyful for in the work that is aligned with your purpose, find small victories to celebrate, find things to be grateful for and to love, in the pursuit of your purpose. Ensure that the activities, training, practice, hard work that is involved in pursuing your purpose is always a joyful, loving and gratitude-filled experience and in so doing you know you are working in the same manner as would your higher-self, and that you are in fullest alignment with your Ideal Parallel World.

DAY 264: You have one responsibility this day and every day. Your greatest responsibility is singular: you must make daily progress toward fulfilling your life's purpose.

DAY 265: Your grandest ambitions change every cell in your body. To move in the direction of your Ideal World is to move in the direction of your purpose. To commence this journey is to be instantly transformed.

DAY 266: View the world before you as an external projection from your own eyes, and know that the world before you is your own to shape and create as you choose. This is how great your power shall be as you approach your Ideal Parallel World. To realize that the world you see through your own eyes is the primary relevant perspective, is to shift worlds.

DAY 267: You shall fall fifty times before you are successful, but success shall be achieved because you keep getting back up. If you decide now that you can handle fifty major falls, and personal injury, and still keep getting up, if you decide now that your dream is worth the struggle and the pain and the disequilibrium and the joy, then right now, you just shifted worlds.

DAY 268: Practice moving towards or away from things as an easy method to shift your life trajectory and therefore to shift your world. Try a move towards social interaction not away from it. Move towards networking not away from it. Move towards structure not away from it.

DAY 269: Focus is most powerful. Your ability to shift your world is highly correlated with your ability to focus.

Day 270: Stop hitting yourself. Only your own blows can keep you from arriving at your Ideal Parallel World.

Day 271: You are a slave to animal instincts until you learn to connect with your subconscious.

Day 272: Allow your destiny to unfold.

Day 273: Allow your powers of attraction to have their effect.

Day 274: Live your life boldly or live as a coward, but do not do both. Select one, now.

Day 275: The outcome does not concern you – focus on the steps required to move towards that which you desire most. Know the desired outcome and know that the joy from achieving the desired outcome must be felt in the present moment.

Day 276: Pay attention to the answers received in silence – all else is noise.

Day 277: Your life is being created based on your persistent pattern of thinking. Learn to think in different ways. The greatest of ways to think is a focused thinking on opportunities and a focus on attaining that which is desired.

Day 278: What is the 80/20 rule? Think on the many ways the 80/20 rule applies to achieving your purpose.

Day 279: Our thoughts alter our direction. Thought processes are what determine our lives. Our view of things is what separates one man from another. Our decisions. Our reactions. Our handling of matters that unfold.

Day 280: Pay attention to the lessons in your life. All experiences are lessons. *"Lessons are repeated until they are learned."* Some people spend an entire lifetime repeating the same lesson.

Day 281: Pay attentions to the lessons in other peoples' lives. Learn from their successes and learn from their failures. Whenever the lesson of another enters your frame of awareness this means that the lesson is being provided to you – it may be provided either as a brand new lesson or as a review of a lesson you have already taken. Learn from all your lessons, use lesson reviews to become a master in this realm.

Day 282: Changing yourself changes the world. By focusing on the internal, on the self, you are able to affect external circumstances. Understand that there is no scenario that is unaffected by you.

Day 283: The mythical 'sword of Gryffindor' only takes in that which makes it stronger, and it is therefore able to destroy great evil. What about you? What do you take in from the experiences of your day? Do you take in suggestions by others that you are weak? Do you take in insults? Do you internalize others' prejudice? Do you listen to that which does not serve your growth?

Day 284: Create and master a system for lifelong education. Knowing that your education shall never cease.

Day 285: Mimic the posture of the successful people you admire. This captures the essence of their force and shall immediately shift your world.

Day 286: There are no possible limitations to your achievements. Any apparent constraint on performance can be overcome by alterations to your environment, mindset, and physical conditioning. You have within your power the ability to alter these three variables in a manner that will lead to improved performance and additional expansion of these variables.

DAY 287: Accept full responsibility for your mistakes whilst knowing that having made mistakes you are now more qualified than ever to succeed in similar circumstances.

DAY 288: At this time in human existence the possibility to rise up and achieve success is available to every individual willing to use time and strategic planning to his advantage. The key is to develop a strategy that is focused on developing oneself so that one is best poised to provide unique benefits to as many people as possible.

DAY 289: Never be weak. Never have shame. Yes, accept responsibility for your wrongdoing, accept that you have fallen victim to your temporary limitations, but never allow yourself to be defeated in your own mind. Keep moving forward; never dwell on weakness.

Day 290: Find those among your peers who will speak to you with the greatest candor. You need, as friends, those will speak to you directly with no attempt to sugarcoat the truth.

Day 291: Laugh at yourself ten times every day. When you misstep and are having a day filled with errors, laugh without ceasing.

Day 292: You have two responsibilities in this life. The first is to decide what shall be your purpose. The second is to wield every force at your disposal to achieve it.

Day 293: Greatness is a skill, it must be practiced like all skills. Even if, at this point in time, you lack access to the opportunity to do nationally great things, or corporate-wide great things, you can practice doing everyday things in a great way. By so doing, you shall attract to you the opportunity to do greater and grander things. Practice small acts of greatness.

Day 294: Never shall you give up. This is the entire key to winning. Even if it is over, then you shall name it the battle and move forward towards winning the war.

DAY 295: Use language like a magic wand. Know that every word, and every sentence, is the casting of a spell, with the ability to alter your world and the world of others. Every sentence has consequence.

DAY 296: It is your strengths and your unique competitive advantages that shall bring you assuredly to greatness. Focus on bolstering your strengths ten times more than you focus on reducing your weaknesses.

DAY 297: Today you shall work on your purpose as if all that you have built up is at stake. Today you shall work on achieving your purpose as if a lack of effort or a failure to give every effort, will destroy you. Today you must work as though all you did in your existence shall count for naught, and that this day is what will determine the realization or failure to achieve your purpose. And then tomorrow you shall do the same, and then the next day, and then the next, and then the next, and then you shall rest – and it shall be revealed to you that this was how you created the universe, this was how you created your Ideal Parallel World.

DAY 298: You shall be most rewarded for your service when such service aligns with your purpose.

Day 299: Your inner voice connects you to your highest self. Listen to that inner voice. Know the Ideal World you imagine is real and that you are moving to it with certainty.

Day 300: You can attain all that you desire whilst adding value to others. Your arrival at your Ideal Parallel World is cause for celebration for all humanity, and your success adds value to all humanity. Rejoice, for you are certain to win.

Thank You for reading 'Your World Shifts.'

Realize that you are now at an entirely different level of performance and potentiality.
Realize that you are greater now than at any other point in your life.
Realize that you have accelerated your advance to your Ideal Parallel World.

At times, it is easy to overlook our own progress, this is not one of those times - take a moment to reflect on just how far you have come and on just how much progress you have made, take a moment to reflect on just how great your potential is at this moment. Thank you for being a part of this co-creation. We did it!

Feel free to email me with any questions or comments at: KevinLMichel@Gmail.com.

If you enjoyed this journey I would be tremendously grateful if you could positively rate this book on Amazon and share it with your closest friends and family. If you can take the moment to do this, I promise you that I will be around for decades to come, learning more each day, and providing you with powerful insights that will allow us both to continue to co-create and continue to shift this world, like never before.

This has been fun! Thank You!

Sincerely, Kevin L. Michel.

Social Media (#MTPW):

www.Twitter.com/KevinLMichel
www.Instagram.com/KevinLMichel_author
www.Facebook.com/MovingThroughParallelWorlds
www.Amazon.com/author/michel
www.Facebook.com/KevinMichel

Sources

1. Anthony Robbins - Various Workshops

2. The Law of Success in Sixteen Lessons - Napoleon Hill

3. The Alchemist - Paolo Coelho

4. The Teachings of Abraham - Esther Hicks - Various Live Performances

5. The University of Success - Og Mandino

6. Moving Through Parallel Worlds to Achieve Your Dreams - Kevin L. Michel

7. The Science of Winning Love - Kevin L. Michel

8. The Greatest Success in the World - Og Mandino

9. How Successful People Think - John C. Maxwell

10. Mastery - Robert Greene

11. Anatomy of the Spirit - Caroline Myss, PH.D.

Printed in Great Britain
by Amazon